G000243724

# SIXTIE

home decoration and furnishings from the 1960s

PUBLISHED BY MIDDLESEX UNIVERSITY PRESS

# CONTENTS

# INTRODUCTION

In 1957 Prime Minister Harold Macmillan declared, 'Let us be frank about it: most of our people have never had it so good'. The pursuit of affluence and a general levelling up of material wealth in society characterised the aspirations of the 1960s.

In 1961 the Parker Morris Report, *Homes for Today and Tomorrow*, proposed building standards that would ensure that Macmillan's comments were true for all new housing, both public and private. The report's recommendations for more space, more heating, and more power points set the agenda for domestic design. By the middle of the decade there was almost no difference between a house built by a local authority and one built by property developers such as SPAN and Wates. The open planning and picture windows that had characterised the wealthier new homes of the 50s became the dominant building style of the 1960s. Spacious open-plan living rooms contrasted with small bedrooms, provided with fitted cupboards. Spending transferred from bedrooms to kitchens as the concept of the fitted kitchen,

*Housing and the GLC, GLC, 1967*
*In general, innovations in housing standards and architecture during the 60s originated in public housing. This led to a convergence between the public and private sectors except in respect of the environments surrounding developments. Greater London Council estates were often bare and open in comparison to those of the private sector developer SPAN, which had a policy of building on sites with mature trees and shrubs. This is a Greater London Council estate at Farnborough.*

JMR 699

BADDA 20905

Good Housekeeping, July 1961
The number of larger houses being built
declined steadily throughout the decade. Their
styling remained rooted in a conservative late-
50s 'contemporary' idiom and relied on
'affluent' features like prominently placed
double garages, large balconies and extra
bathrooms to convey status.

with its white goods such as fridges and washing machines, developed from a luxury to a necessity. Increasing car ownership led to the development of the three-storey 'town-house' on small urban sites, with a garage, toilet and utility room on the ground floor and the living area on the first floor.

The aesthetics of Modernism overarched the decade. In art, this was manifested in the form of abstraction, beginning with Expressionism and later developing into the rigid geometry of Op and Pop Art; art had a strong influence on design. In architecture, Modernism was chiefly manifest in the open-plan style and with this came a concern for clean sharp lines, minimal but exact detailing and the use of large areas of oiled wood, white paint and exposed brick or stonework. In design, Modernist styling initially took its lead from architecture and there is a close fit between the Scandinavian-influenced 'teak' furniture of the early 60s and the interior look of Modernist architecture. After 1966 design became increasingly influenced by Pop Art and its associated values of fun and disposability.

So, in new homes, the 60s began with a rather stripped-back, architect-led aesthetic: built-in furniture in bedrooms and kitchens, simply shaped room dividers and sideboards, a broad use of colour and little pattern. In the latter part of the decade there was a reaction against this functional Modernism; the consumerism and individualism that characterised the 'new generation' led to a more fashion-driven aesthetic. There was also the beginning of an adaptation of previous styles and exotic cultures, which produced colourful and fantastic interiors that mirrored the escapism of the 'counter culture'. The new generation of homemakers also began to re-inhabit the inner suburbs of cities and re-vamp their predominantly Victorian properties.

# FURNITURE

Until around 1966 the dominant fashionable style was 'Scandinavian', with its mixture of fairly conventional dining suites and low, slim sofas and armchairs. Furniture frames were often of oiled woods and upholstery was narrow in section. Upright wall furniture systems in exotic hardwoods were a newer element in the Scandinavian style, beginning to supplant the previously ubiquitous long, low sideboard.

A popular, American-style, item of furniture was the 'masculine' lounger — a large, high-backed chair, frequently accompanied by a footstool. The archetype of this was the Eames recliner, though these were rare.

Because most bedrooms in new houses were small, space-saving built-in units faced with veneers became an established norm and had the effect of reducing the market for traditional bedroom suites. Where suites continued to be produced, as in the G-Plan range, they were designed as free-standing versions of their built-in cousins. Children's bedrooms often featured bunk beds.

After 1965 a more Mediterranean-influenced style appeared, pioneered in Terence Conran's new Habitat shops. Habitat was innovative in offering furniture off-the-shelf and later by mail order. But more important was the style (and life style) it provided, suggestive of a synthesis of al fresco dining and La Dolce Vita. The look relied on simple, rustic designs in materials like pine, stained wood and rush. At the same time the use of plastics became a common feature of furniture, often overtly celebrating the shiny smoothness that was the unique quality of the material. By the end of the 60s there was a rediscovery of Art Deco, Art Nouveau and Victorian furniture. This began as a sort of 'dressing up' but soon became a more wistful historicism.

This shift in attitudes in the late 60s was accelerated by the development of less structured, disposable furniture, such as bean bags, which retailed through the new off-the-shelf boutiques that made interior design as varied as fashion.

**ILLUSTRATION 1**

Good Housekeeping, *March 1963*

**ILLUSTRATION 2**

*Catalogue for Finmar Furniture, 1962*

**ILLUSTRATION 1** Middle-market, middle-class furniture combined the low, floating, horizontality of Modern styling with the reassuring traditions of overstuffed and buttoned upholstery. Teak gradually acquired the connotations of conservative solidity previously ascribed to mahogany. In larger homes, the big spaces created by open-planning were modulated by the introduction of split levels between dining and lounge areas.

**ILLUSTRATION 2** In the early 60s, Modern furniture was commonly ordered from catalogues. Scandinavian design was widely produced and well marketed for export through companies like Finmar, whose products were available in wide range of qualities and prices. These factors, amongst others, helped Scandinavian Modernism dominate the 'good design' market in Britain in the early and mid 60s.

**ILLUSTRATION 3** By the end of the 60s, furniture had become much more driven by fashion and the recognition of new consumer types within the family. Even do-it-yourself furniture felt obliged to recognise teenagers. In line with the current convention, it equated youth with bright colour.

BADDA 1482

**ILLUSTRATION 4**
*Catalogue for Finmar Furniture, 1962*

BADDA 2789

**ILLUSTRATION 4** The open-living aesthetic and the unfashionability of case furniture, such as chests of drawers, led to the development of room dividers, which combined the functions of earlier items of living area furniture.

**ILLUSTRATION 5**
*Advertisement from* Homes
and Gardens, *December 1966*

**ILLUSTRATION 5** The three-piece suite was challenged by its association with pre-modern suburban values and manufacturers tried to re-invent what had previously been an expensive necessity in every respectable home. The main focus of this redesigning was the armchair, which was often restyled to appeal to men by combining overstuffed comfort with a suggestion of the boss's office and the Bond villain.

**ILLUSTRATION 6** Along with the built-in aesthetic came the idea of modularisation and furniture systems. The item on the left combines wardrobes, chests of drawers and shelves.

**ILLUSTRATION 6**
*Storage, G Salmon, 1967*

**ILLUSTRATION 7**
Homes and Gardens, *January 1964*

Reproduced courtesy of Homes and Gardens

**ILLUSTRATION 7** Until the end of the 60s most furniture sold in Britain was bought in suites, often by hire purchase, and delivered twelve weeks after order. Equally, the tradition of buying furniture only once in a lifetime persisted. These factors led to a persistence of the conservative, vaguely Regency, styling that was popular throughout the 20th century.

**ILLUSTRATION 8** In the bedroom, as in the living room, the built-in furniture that was an element of Modernism threatened older furnishing styles. Bedroom suites were designed to look 'built-in' by virtue of their use of a grid design, flat undecorated surfaces and small handles.

**ILLUSTRATION 8**
Catalogue for Remploy Bedroom Furniture, 1970

BADDA 1368 Reproduced courtesy of Remploy

**ILLUSTRATION 9** A major element in the Modernist style was the combination of minimalism and luxury. In many British homes this idea was represented by system furnishing. Items such as bureaux or sideboards, made into units which hung from battens on the wall, concentrated elements of living-room furniture into one area. These units were given the luxury they lacked in their form by the use of expensive and exotic hardwoods such as teak or, more rarely, rosewood.

## ILLUSTRATION 10

Habitat. Creative Living By Post, *1969*

a **CAMPUS LOWBACK CHAIR** in cyclamen upholstery with a
  white lacquered frame. Detailed on page 7.
  091164                                   **£13 10 0**
b **CAMPUS FOOTSTOOL** finished to match the above. As with
  the entire Campus range, finishes and fabrics are available from
  those displayed on page 11. Measures 15 × 28 × 23½ ins.
  091312                                     **£ 9 15 0**
c **CAMPUS HIGHBACK CHAIR**, illustrated here in an orange
  upholstery with a red frame and in indigo blue with a brown
  frame. Further details on page 6.
  091155                                     **£14 19 6**

**CAMPUS** furniture is delivered to you in a carton, unassembled. It is extremely simple to assemble, the only tool required being an Allen key, which is, of course, provided, with full assembly instructions. Complete assembly should take no more than 10 minutes.

When ordering Campus furniture state frame finish and upholstery colour clearly. See page 11 for details.

**ILLUSTRATION 10** Habitat, like Chippendale, brought style to the provinces. The simple Modernist aesthetics of the mid 60s were ideal for self-assembly. The mail order catalogue meant that fashionable furniture could be delivered anywhere in the country.

**ILLUSTRATION 11** Stylistically, Habitat pioneered the move away from Scandinavian Modernism toward a more colourful and informal, 'Mediterranean', peasant-inspired, simplicity which was increasingly popular from the mid 60s.

## ILLUSTRATION 11

Habitat. Creative Living By Post, *1969*

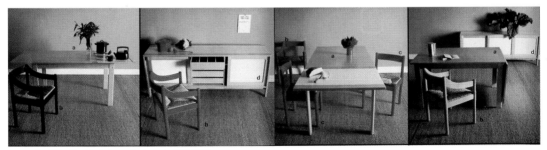

Private collection

**ILLUSTRATION 12**
English Style, *Mary Gilliat*, 1967

**ILLUSTRATION 12** This illustration of Terence Conran's house reflects his mid-60s taste for rugged minimalism combined with timeless rural simplicty. The effect is created by the combination of country antiques and modern versions of peasant styles in beech or pine.

**ILLUSTRATION 13** By the close of the decade the move of fashionable homemakers back to inner-city terraces and cottages led to a revival of interest in Victorian interiors. But this did not extend to a liking for dark colours - many pieces of Victorian and Regency furniture were painted in bright gloss colours.

**ILLUSTRATION 13**
English Style, *Mary Gilliat*, 1967

Private collection

# CURTAINS AND UPHOLSTERY

Larger living areas, a reduction in the amount and scale of furniture and an increase in glazed areas gave curtains, nets and carpets a prominent decorative role.

The large picture windows of open-plan homes and the development of commercial screen-printing in the early years of the 60s encouraged the use of big, bold designs and textures. Early in the decade firms such as Edinburgh Weavers commissioned designs from architects and artists, resulting in a cultured style that referred to Abstract Expressionism and classical architecture and employed very large repeats. In the mid 60s this gave way to smaller repeats and more naturalistic, but still abstract, motifs and to some Op-Art-inspired patterns. By the end of the decade, graphic design and Pop Art values began to dominate and bold, colourful, floral motifs emerged, epitomised by the prints of the Finnish firm, Marimekko. Colours, which for much of the decade were in dark-hued complementary tones, after 1967 became increasingly bright, contrasting and artificial.

Initially, window fabrics were often textural, ranging from self-consciously slubby linens and loosely woven wools to sheer nylon nets, but towards the end of the decade there was less emphasis on texture in favour of supergraphic screen-print effects on flat cotton. Blinds became an increasingly acceptable alternative to curtains. Venetian blinds in pastel colours were popular in the early 60s, changing to a taste for white or primary colours and flat cotton roller blinds towards 1970.

Upholstery fabrics began the decade in a tasteful architectural mode of rough textures and abstract forms and ended with designs based in Pop culture - brightly coloured screen-prints, fashion-fabric-related elephant cord or 'sexy' leather and PVC. At the same time, there was a continuing taste for using traditional quasi-folk weaves such as Welsh Tapestry or the more exotic seagrass for chair seats and place mats.

**ILLUSTRATION 1**

Ideal Home Householder's Guide Volume 2,
Decoration and Furnishing, 1966

**ILLUSTRATIONS 1 & 2** The big
picture windows that were a
standard feature of modern 60s
homes often occupied the space of
an entire wall. Many people used
net curtains for privacy in addition
to textured or patterned curtains.
Designs were often large-scale.
Lightweight fabrics minimised
'bulking up' when they were open
during the day. Conventionally,
curtains were mounted on tracks
behind shallow, bare wood pelmets.

**ILLUSTRATION 3** The most
dynamic area of domestic styling
was in printed fabrics. An increase
in the number of designers coming
through the new art schools and
the widespread introduction of
screen-printing meant that every
nuance of 60s design found itself
represented in furnishing fabrics.
These designs from 1964 show the
immediate influence of Pop and Op
Art as well as the beginnings of
interest in peasant cultures and
graphic processes.

**ILLUSTRATION 2**

Homes and Gardens, June 1964

**ILLUSTRATION 3**
House and Garden, *March 1964*

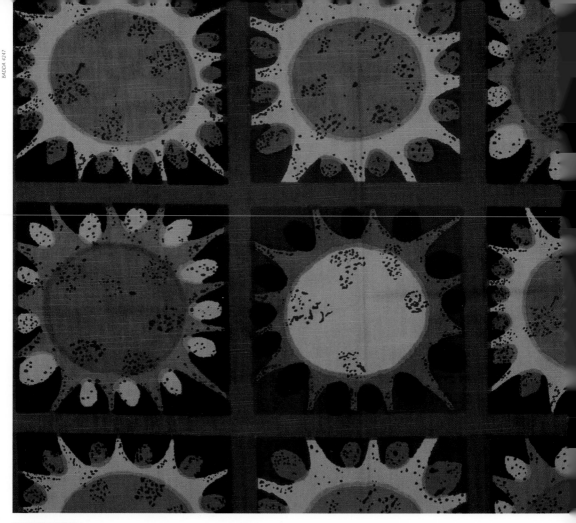

**ILLUSTRATION 4**

*Screen-printed cotton, about 1960*

**ILLUSTRATION 4** This Scandinavian design, *Plexus*, is by Sven Fristedt for Borås. It mirrors contemporary ceramic designs for tiled tables and coffee services as well as jewellery designs. The homology between designs in different areas of domestic product was a result of the Bauhaus-style training given in the new art schools in Britain and Europe.

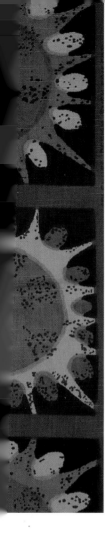

ILLUSTRATION 5
*Printed textile, later 1960s*

BADDA 4250

**ILLUSTRATION 5** At the end of the 60s, a revival of interest in the art of the fin de siècle, Art Nouveau and Art Deco had begun to affect commercial design. This fabric combines the contemporary taste for simplified patterns with references to the patterns of the Austrian Secessionist movement. White became a popular background colour and the dominant paint colour for the fashionable home.

**ILLUSTRATION 6** Throughout the 60s, floral designs remained popular but the old naturalism and diagonally designed repeats gave way to simplified, naive designs based on linear grids.

BADDA 3201

ILLUSTRATION 6
*Printed textile, later 1960s*

**ILLUSTRATION 7**
Good Housekeeping Home Encyclopaedia, 1968

**ILLUSTRATION 7** Many of the new window shapes in modern homes, particularly the long, shallow, fixed lights mounted high in the wall, were unsuitable for curtains. Venetian blinds in pastel colours and, later, fabric roller blinds, offered alternative coverings. By the late 60s, roller blinds were a popular choice for any window but especially in bathrooms, kitchens, landings and toilets.

**ILLUSTRATION 8** Even in modern homes many people preferred traditional 'chintzy' floral designs, but these were now treated in a light and sketchy way in keeping with the general reduction of pattern in the interior.

**ILLUSTRATION 9** The Finnish company, Marimekko, represented the new face of Scandinavian design. Unlike many British companies, it was a self-consciously low-volume producer more akin to a fashion company than a mass-market fabric producer. The large-scale pattern of this roller blind is typical of Marimekko's art-based aesthetic.

BADDA 2090.1

**ILLUSTRATION 10** Upholstery fabrics were usually textured weaves rather than prints. Loose-woven hessian effects and tweedy bouclé, in white or strong colours, were particularly popular at first. By the end of the 60s, though, plain flatweaves or corduroys, either in white or very dark colours, were becoming fashionable.

**ILLUSTRATION 9**

*Design, August 1968*

BADDA 3271.5  Reproduced courtesy of the Design Council

**ILLUSTRATION 10**

CoID Contract Catalogue, *Design Index, 1969/1970*

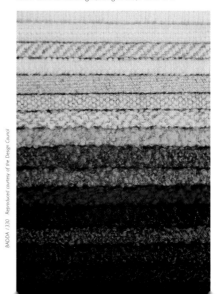

BADDA 1330  Reproduced courtesy of the Design Council

**ILLUSTRATION 11**

*Linen tea towel, 1970*

BADDA 4028

**ILLUSTRATION 11** The tea towel was a major medium of experimental pattern design in the 60s. In this example, by Jocelyn Anderson, a traditional Chinese pheasant motif is brought up-to-date by the use of the Pop aesthetic of separating decorative elements and employing bright synthetic colours.

# WALLS AND PAINT

The relative absence of furniture from interiors gave new significance to the finish of the walls and other surfaces. The decade began with an interest in textured effects, such as hessian (either real or imitation), and ended with, on the one hand, smooth patterned finishes inspired by plastics and Pop culture and, on the other, a rediscovery of stripped wood and heavy Victorian fabrics and patterns.

Exposed brick was an increasingly popular wall finish in living areas; for dining areas tongue-and-groove redwood pine created an instantly 'Scandinavian' effect that complemented open planning. These surfaces contrasted with the more synthetic finishes in adjacent kitchen areas.

The new Brilliant White emulsion emerged as the dominant modern wall finish. Strong colours were often used in limited areas as a counterpoint. The range of emulsion colours increased over the decade; fashionable 'highlight' colours changed from cold hues in the early 60s through warmer, earthy colours, such as Thames green, in the mid 60s, to primary and synthetic colours, such as shocking pink, as the influence of Pop culture took hold.

Patterned wallpaper was less popular than it had been as a material for entire rooms, although small areas were often used as highlights. This way of using wallpaper was encouraged by the introduction of ranges of co-ordinated papers and fabrics. By the end of the decade, new production techniques that allowed a variety of textures and finishes to appear on one paper, led to some 'glamorous' designs, such as metallic stripes or Pop-inspired psychedelia. Newly developed vinyl-coated papers were washable and so were particularly useful for kitchens and bathrooms. Abstract textured papers, 'artex' textured paint and woodchip papers, all of which could be painted, were popular throughout the period.

There was also a vogue for tiling tabletops, and even the walls above fireplaces, with tiles that echoed the patterns of contemporary fabrics.

**ILLUSTRATIONS 1 & 2** In general, most of the 60s was marked by the dominance of the new Brilliant White emulsion as the basic wall colour, highlighted by restricted areas of colour. There was a marked trend, following Scandinavian and Brutalist precedents, towards bare or white-painted brick walls in living areas. In kitchens, dining rooms and bathrooms, again following Scandinavian style, there was a taste for pine tongue-and-groove cladding. This continued in kitchens and bathrooms into the 70s.

**ILLUSTRATION 1**
English Style, Mary Gilliat, 1967

**ILLUSTRATION 2**
Good Housekeeping, February 1961

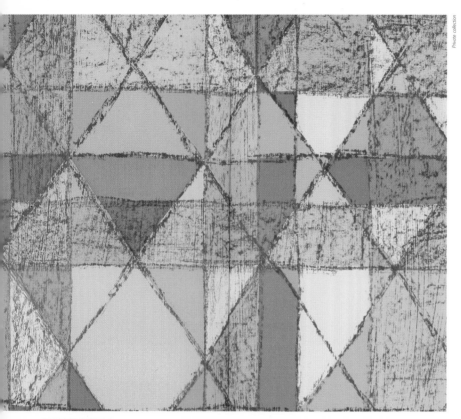

**ILLUSTRATION 3**

*Wallpaper, produced by Shand Kydd, 1963*

**ILLUSTRATION 3** In the early 60s, wallpapers in modern houses were frequently used to highlight one wall, balancing the large curtains at the picture windows. This pattern, designed by Tessa Hagity, recreates the muted tones, abstract patterning and 'linen' feel of late-50s and early-60s modernist curtains and the rather masculine formality of this architect-led style.

**ILLUSTRATIONS 4 & 5** In the early to mid 60s there was a fashion for wallpapers that featured self-consciously artistic, hand-wrought, designs by famous artists and designers. These patterns predated Pop and were in the spirit and scale of Abstract Expressionism and European Art Brut, which were popular with architects. Such designs were used to make one room or wall a special feature of the home. Reproductions of famous art works, such as Picasso's Guernica, could be used in the same way.

**ILLUSTRATION 5**

Schema *wallpaper, by Peter Smithson, from the* Palladio Magnus *range, produced by Lightbown Aspinall, 1960*

This is a young wallpaper.
It isn't going to please everybody.
Your old Aunt Emily will probably hate it.
She also hates mini-skirts, fast cars and Pop.
We aren't trying to please Aunt Emily.

Crown washable wallpapers make a bathroom brighter. They're young, fashionable and full of colour. What's more, they're practical. Wet, splashed or stained, a quick wash-over leaves them fresh and beautiful as new. Come to think of it, don't Crown washables sound a good bet for all your rooms? They're certainly dependable. One of the reasons why more than half the homes in Britain decorate with Crown paints and wallpapers.

count on Crown with confidence

'Scene' no. SC120 (washable) at 13/- per roll (excl. tax)

Reproduced courtesy of CWV Group Ltd

**ILLUSTRATION 6** The brief moment of Flower Power in 1968 spawned an outburst of floral prints that followed the lead of fashion fabric designs - densely packed flowers in strong pastel colours, arranged in a seemingly random pattern on a brilliant white ground.

**ILLUSTRATION 7** Commercial paints were still in the dark ages during the 60s - many colours combined coldness with a synthetic appearance, while pale colours often had too much white in them. Coloured paint was used mostly for kitchen and bathroom walls. In the early 60s the pastel blues and yellows of the 50s were still popular but by the middle of the decade there was a growing vogue for acidic yellows and hotter reds and oranges on walls, often in combination with sludgy greeny browns. Gloss, sometimes coloured, was used for woodwork and there was a marked fashion for bright front doors.

ILLUSTRATION 7

Ripolin paint chart, 1965

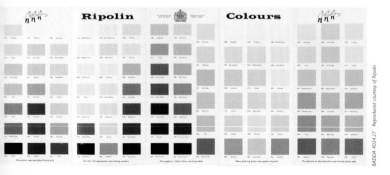

**Ripolin** **Colours**

BADDA 4024.27   Reproduced courtesy of Ripolin

# FLOORING

Many new homes of the 60s were equipped with under-floor heating, which required hard, uncarpeted floors. These floors, often of parquet or thermoplastic tiles, acted as a good foil for rugs. So, at the end of the decade, did the stripped pine boards of the newly modish refurbished Georgian and Victorian houses. Until the late 60s colourful, long-haired Scandinavian Rya rugs, with their large-scale abstract patterns were very fashionable. Later, Greek flokatis (which were similarly shaggy but white all over) and oriental kelims became popular. The different functional areas of open-plan rooms were often indicated by different floor coverings — rugs by sofas and harder materials, such as seagrass tiled mats, in dining areas.

Fitted carpet was available increasingly cheaply and often covered the entire floor area of a house; different grades were used for different rooms. Plain colours in a variety of assertive textures, from hard to shaggy, were popular throughout the decade. Tintawn whipcord was a favourite for living areas as it was hardwearing and suited the textured modern interiors of the earlier part of the decade. Upstairs, longer-haired carpets in pale, neutral, tones were used to convey a sense of luxury. Most redolent of the period was shag pile, a long-haired broadloom carpet made possible by new bonding materials. Pattern, though, did persist in traditionally made woven Wilton carpets. They began the decade in subdued, rather Expressionistic abstract styles, giving way later to floral designs in a format similar to that of the popular fabrics - simple grid repeats and bright, simply stylised flowers, creating a graphic, rather than a naturalistic, effect.

Bathrooms had more functional flooring, such as cork or, more commonly, patterned thermoplastic tiles or, more expensively, linoleum. Bathroom carpet was rubber-backed, often shaggy and open-woven, in pastel shades; there were similar washable toilet carpets.

**ILLUSTRATION I**

*Advertisement from House and Garden,
March 1964*

**ILLUSTRATION 2**

Colour in Interior Decoration, *R Smithells, 1966*

Private collection

**ILLUSTRATION I** Wall-to-wall carpeting was the most popular flooring material. The use of synthetic materials and glues brought down the price and it became available in widths of up to five metres. In the early 60s, fitted carpets emulated the density and plushness of traditional wool carpet. Colours were generally strong so as not to show the dirt.

**ILLUSTRATION 2** This muted design follows trends established in the 50s that stayed popular in modern homes throughout the 60s. The success of such designs lies in their illusion of texture (also seen on curtains and walls), which was used as a counterpoint to the wide open spaces of open-plan. By the close of the decade this would have been considered a very safe, conservative design.

**ILLUSTRATION 3** As in other areas of domestic design, the carpet industry attempted to keep up with the fast-changing trends of the 60s. The striking pattern of this Op-Art-inspired carpet is set off by the use of white almost everywhere else.

ILLUSTRATION 3

House and Garden Guide to
Interior Decoration, 1967

Private collection    John Wingrove / House and Garden ©The Condé Nast Publications Ltd

**ILLUSTRATION 4**
Colour in Interior Decoration, *R Smithells, 1966*

**ILLUSTRATION 4** The apparently large floor spaces created by lighter and sparser furnishing gave an opportunity for a greater use of pattern in fitted carpets. However, such designs tended to dominate the room and so they were rarely used in the living areas of houses.

**ILLUSTRATION 5** By the end of the 60s, coarse 'berber' or corded fitted carpets in light colours were

**ILLUSTRATION 5**
House and Garden Guide to
Interior Decoration, 1967

Private collection

**ILLUSTRATION 6**
Colour in Interior Decoration, R Smithells, 1966

very fashionable but the most chic
of all was white shag pile. This
replicated the effect of a long-
haired rug on a room-size scale.

**ILLUSTRATION 6** Many architects
and designers specified hard floor
surfaces in living areas because this
was a 'quality' finish for concrete
floors. Parquet flooring, made up of
small hardwood tiles glued onto
the floor below, was very stylish
and relatively cheap and so was
used extensively in the living areas
of the modern town-houses built
for the middle classes.

**ILLUSTRATION 8**
Colour in Interior Decoration, *R Smithells, 1966*

**ILLUSTRATION 7**
Colour in Interior Decoration, *R Smithells, 1966*

**ILLUSTRATION 7** The arty handcraft look of 'Scandinavian' rya-style rugs went well with the hard floor finishes of many modernist homes of the 60s.

**ILLUSTRATION 8** One essential element of the Scandinavian style that lasted well into the 60s was the taste for simple natural materials. These tessellated sea-grass rugs were cheap and popular as a covering for floors in dining rooms and kitchens – not least because they smelt of summer straw.

**ILLUSTRATION 9**
ColD Contract Catalogue, *Design Index 1969/1970*

**ILLUSTRATION 9** Plastics played an increasingly important role in the 60s house. Thermoplastic vinyl tiles quickly replaced lino as the material of choice for covering high traffic areas such as halls and wet areas like bathrooms. The shiny appearance of these tiles also made them a popular floor material for living areas in modern homes where parquet was considered too expensive.

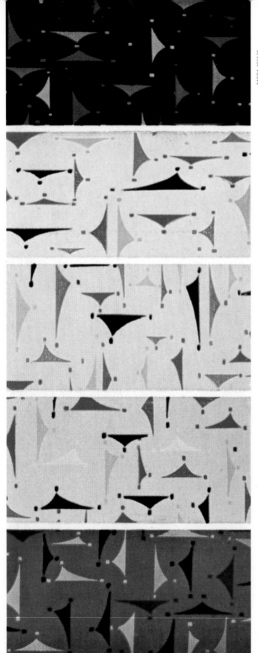

BADDA 40232S

**ILLUSTRATION 10**
*Catalogue for Krommenie Coloretta*
*Thermoplastic Flooring, 1965*

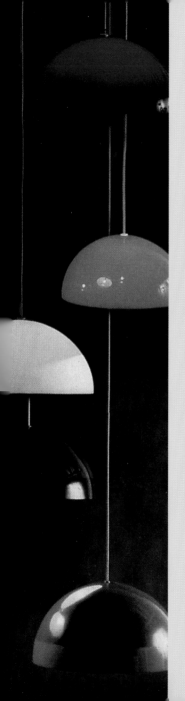

# LIGHTING

The Parker Morris report advised the provision of more power sockets in the home. This, together with the new availability of higher wattage bulbs, led to major changes in domestic lighting. The old hierarchy of a central ceiling light augmented by standard lamps and table lamps was replaced by a much more dramatic and flexible approach.

In kitchens, work surfaces were brightly illuminated by strip lights set below eye level while high-level fluorescent tubes provided an overall strong light. In contrast, living areas benefited from the development of spot and track lighting and silvered bulbs. These could deliver pools of light to specific points while keeping the general levels low, providing drama and a sense of scale. A new form of standard lamp – a sweeping metal arm which arched over a chair from behind – was an alternative to the more traditional upright version.

In bedrooms, uplighters and downlighters began to replace bedside lamps and here, as elsewhere, the new dimmer switches made light much more controllable. In dining areas, ceiling lights above the table were often mounted on counterbalanced mechanisms, which enabled them to be raised or lowered depending on the intimacy of the occasion.

Spot lamps (not spot bulbs), whether used as standards or on tracks or as wall or ceiling lights, were minimal in form. Popular finishes were coloured enamel or, later, anodised aluminium, coloured from bronze to gold. These materials were used also for the large dining-room shades that were designed to combine a bright downlight with a softer penumbra of ambient light. By the end of the decade these expensive shades were replaced by hemispherical or Chinese-hat shades made of metal, coloured plastic or paper. Throughout the house, 'Japanese' spherical paper lanterns, sometimes as much as a metre in diameter, were an enduring favourite. Toward the end of the period, printed fabric or rattan 'mobcap' shades suited the emergent softer, nostalgic interiors.

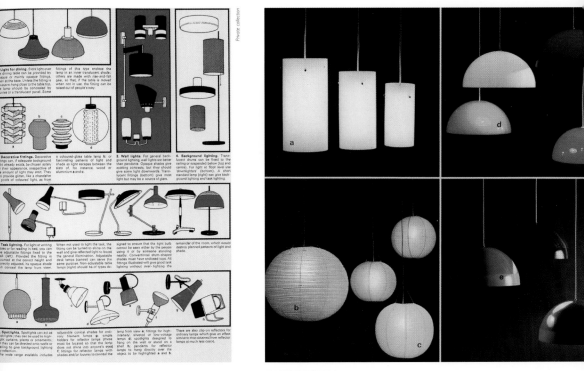

**ILLUSTRATION I**
Book of Home Decoration, *edited by Elizabeth Gundrey, 1968*

**ILLUSTRATION 2**
Habitat. Creative Living By Post, *1969*

**ILLUSTRATION I** Because of innovations in lighting technology, new designs and the high standards of provision set by the Parker Morris report of 1961, there was a profusion of novel lighting appliances in the late 60s. Lighting became an area of aesthetic choice rather than a utility with a shade.

**ILLUSTRATION 2** The central light remained a feature of most houses. The minimalism of form and bright colours of these shades were in line with the general minimalism of electrical design at the time. Modern lampshades rarely had a smooth stylistic match with other elements in a room design.

**ILLUSTRATION 3**

Habitat. Creative Living By Post, 1969

**ILLUSTRATION 3** Before Habitat, well-designed lamp fittings were expensive and hard to obtain but these cheap copies of Scandinavian fittings brought fashionable advanced lighting effects within reach of the first time homemaker. In common with many fashion products of the day, these fittings were not expected to last long and they would be replaced by a new style within a short period.

# TABLE SETTINGS
## for four seasons

HOMES AND GARDENS
GIFT BOOKLET MAY 1964

PRODUCED FOR MELMEX IN ASSOCIATION WITH BRITISH INDUSTRIAL PLASTICS LTD

**HOMES** and gardens

DECEMBER 1966 BOOK OF

## PARTY FOOD AND WINE

**ILLUSTRATION 4** This type of technical, modern, almost streamlined, light fitting went well with the bourgeois respectability of 'Scandinavian' design. Its seriousness and taste ensured its fall from favour as more colourful and youth-oriented designs began to dominate interior design after 1965.

**ILLUSTRATION 5** This kind of lampshade and its close relation, the 'mobcap', became popular in the late 60s. It used fashionable fabric, it was cheap and it fitted in with the emerging nostalgic interior design trends – it was a light but it looked like a furnishing.

**ILLUSTRATION 6** By the late 60s, the generally generous provision of plug sockets throughout the home made more sophisticated lighting possible. Dominant central lighting was becoming unfashionable; a wide range of lower powered, more discreet lamps was developed which could create pools of light rather than an overall ambient brightness.

**ILLUSTRATION 6**

Homes and Gardens Supplement: Up-to-Date Living, *November 1966*

Plug in, switch on

Crabtree's new range of switch socket outlets, fused spur units, and switches incorporates a flush rocker-operated switch. This makes possible a complete matching range with visual indication when in the on position, and a flush face when off. To operate the switch, its lower end is pressed into a recess below the surface of the plate, which brings its upper end out so ON is visible. The units can be obtained with neon indicators.

BADDA 3271.1   Reproduced courtesy of the Design Council

**ILLUSTRATION 7**
Design, February 1968

**ILLUSTRATION 8**
English Style, Mary Gilliat, 1967

Private collection

**ILLUSTRATION 7** In the early 60s, dark brown Bakelite switches and sockets were still widely fitted. But by the end of the decade cheap, standard, white and tastefully neutral designs made electric power an invisible part of the home. At the more glamorous end of the market, the dimmer switch, often combined with track lighting, gave what was thought at the time to be total control over illumination.

**ILLUSTRATION 8** The most minimal lighting design of the 60s was the track-mounted spotlight. This enabled a number of lights to be hidden, almost out of view, and angled to deliver pools of light where needed. Early spots were expensive and, although cheap versions soon became available, track lighting retained its aura of designer smartness.

# FINISHING TOUCHES

At the beginning of the decade the taste was for only a few incidental objects in a room and for combining restrained contemporary items with antiques; by the end of the decade eclectic 'clutter' enjoyed a revival. Everyday objects became more ornamental as the last hangover of austerity passed and there was continuing interest in using items of popular culture and objets trouvés for ornaments. With the increase in central heating, houseplants became more exotic; there was, for instance, a fashion for growing African violets in old carboys.

Early-60s, middle-ground artistic taste favoured the neo-romanticism of artists such as John Piper and Roland Hilder, both of whose paintings and prints were much reproduced. Later on, under the influence of Pop culture, posters became widely available and very popular. They were often displayed in the kitchen.

Design-conscious homeowners might have had stainless steel one-piece cutlery by David Mellor and tableware in the smoothly swooping shapes of 'Scandinavian' design. Ceramics and cookware took on a characteristic boxy or geometric shape that offered a large surface for bold graphic prints, which manufacturers like Midwinter and Portmeirion applied to their wares. Brightly coloured Melamine cups and plates were popular for children and informal occasions, while transparent plastic was used for picnic equipment.

By 1963, eighty-two per cent of households owned a TV and more a radio. The majority of radio and TV cases followed trends in modern furniture; Ferguson televisions of the late 60s, for instance, had cabinets finished in eggshell white or Thames green. The development of transistors enabled firms such as Sony to produce small portable TVs but, at the same time, many people acquired the new larger screens. At the top end of the new hi-fi market, companies such as Quad were evolving a 'technical' appearance, which quickly replaced the cabinet styling of earlier equipment.

**ILLUSTRATION I**

English Style, *Mary Gilliat, 1967*

**ILLUSTRATION I** One particularly British interior design fashion was the minimalist cottage style, seen here in the home of artist William Scott. The stripped-out and white-painted room has been decorated like an art gallery, with choice and understated examples of vernacular antiques alongside a modern sofa, coffee table and armchairs. A few carefully placed lights and small decorative objects complete the effect.

**ILLUSTRATION 2**
Interior Design, *Diana Rowntree, 1964*

**ILLUSTRATION 3**
Colour in Interior Decoration, *R Smithells, 1966*

**ILLUSTRATION 2** By the mid 60s, virtually every home had a TV. As radiant fires gave way to the ambient warmth of central heating, the TV took over from the fireplace as the centre of the home and living-room layouts reflected this. New TVs were designed to be attractive pieces of furniture.

**ILLUSTRATION 3** This room set, with its teak dining table and sideboard, represents a form of early 60s international Modernism. Stainless steel became cheaper at this time but was still expensive enough to be considered suitable as a material for almost every piece of a dining service. Place mats in fabrics like woven grass or rough linen replaced the traditional tablecloths, thus allowing the wood of the table to be seen.

**ILLUSTRATION 5**

*Advertisement from* Good Housekeeping, *March 1962*

# It's SMART to be PRACTICAL

## That's why you'll go for break-resistant Melaware

Melaware brings a splash of sunshine to your table with its range of gay colours. Its simple, tasteful lines echo the best of design. Yet Melaware is more than an ornament. Because it's break-resistant, it stands up to the hurly-burly of the kitchen sink superbly. Melaware pays tribute to your good taste *and* your good sense.

### MELAWARE GUARANTEE
Melaware is guaranteed for 12 months against chipping and cracking in normal domestic household use.
Melaware is made from Melmex Melamine

Send for illustrated brochure and the name of your nearest stockist to MELAWARE LIMITED, 9 Argyll Street, London W1, Telephone Gerrard 9187

BADDA 2090.6

**ILLUSTRATION 4** Throughout the decade, mass manufacturers of ceramics employed modern designers to create lines of 'studio' pottery. The moulded, organic shapes of the 1950s and early 60s gave way to more 'rational', boxy forms. Decoration moved on from hand-painted or transfer motifs to hard-edged screen-printed patterns based in Op and Pop Art. There were also many commercial 'art' wares that featured embossed patterns based on pseudo-ethnic carving. Popular body colours were white or dark blue and earthy greens, reds, oranges and browns.

**ILLUSTRATION 5** While stainless steel became the new material of cutlery, cookware and dining rooms,

**ILLUSTRATION 6**
Ideal Home Householder's Guide, Volume 2:
Decoration and Furnishing, 1966

*Private collection*

Melamine became the new pottery
and the most acceptable face of
plastics in the home. Early-60s
Melaware used bright colours and
the indestructible nature of the
material to challenge the supremacy
of ceramics for crockery. Later, it
became more muted in colour and
semi-matt in texture as part of the
manufacturer's efforts to overcome
the popular view that plastic was a
substitute material.

**ILLUSTRATION 6** One of the
fundamental tropes of Modernist
architecture was the destruction
of the barrier between inside and
outside. In more affluent homes,
open-plan living extended through
the picture windows (often
re-termed patio doors) out to
the patio.

Left: Hoover Convertible has suction dial for carpet and accessory tools

**ILLUSTRATION 8**
Ideal Home Householder's Guide, Volume 2: Decoration and Furnishing, 1966

BADDA 3271.3   Reproduced courtesy of the Design Council

**ILLUSTRATION 7**
Design, June 1968

Hoover Portable is designed for easy transport-ation. Picture above shows its neat storage.

Private collection

**ILLUSTRATION 7** Although interiors were becoming more colourful, expressionistic or nostalgic, electrical items maintained the technicist aesthetic of the early 60s. As more electrical equipment entered the home, it was generally designed to be smaller, blander and more self-effacing. This increasing minimalism was much aided by the widespread adoption of transistor technology in the late 60s. The Trimline telephone is an example of this tendency.

**ILLUSTRATION 8** Vacuum cleaners became ubiquitous in the British home during the 60s. Designers worked on making them lighter and more flexible. Their widespread ownership also encouraged the increasing use of fitted carpet, as they were essential to its

# KITCHENS

In 1961 only five per cent of kitchens met the standards recommended by the Parker Morris report of that year; by the end of the decade those standards had become typical. The report recommended layouts designed to minimise labour, the inclusion of labour-saving equipment such as fridges, washing machines and food mixers, and the provision of sufficient electric points to power them. Parker Morris proposed that kitchens should be fitted with prefabricated storage units in modules 90cm high and 60cm deep. Their doors and drawers were initially made from painted plywood but chipboard, veneered with coloured Formica, soon took over. Worktops were either Formica or stainless steel. Early in the 60s, sinks were often made of enamelled steel and coloured white, cream or a pastel shade, but by the middle of the decade these were giving way to stainless steel. Differences were usually of emphasis and size rather than form. Built-in fridges, hobs, twin ovens and extractor hoods, all designed to fit in with cupboard modules, began to appear in the later 60s. After 1965, as cooking became an affluent spectator sport, luxury kitchens adopted the island layout.

As elsewhere in the house, tastes changed during the decade. Initially, the fashionable architectural style favoured a sleek and rather severe approach – units with recessed handles and smooth steel worktops, illuminated by strip lights, set beneath the shallower wall cupboards above. Cool colours, such as ice blue, were highlighted by white. Later on, a more relaxed look became fashionable. Colours were warmer; work surfaces were edged with natural teak or beech detailing; splash areas were frequently tiled with colourful abstract motifs. By the late 60s a reaction against the overtly modern led to a reinvention of the 'farmhouse' or 'cottage' kitchen and the reinstatement of pine tables and chairs. Manufacturers used oak veneers and faux panelled doors in the attempt to give their units a 'farmhouse' look.

**ILLUSTRATION 1**

House and Garden, *March 1964*

**ILLUSTRATION 2**

Kitchens: Plan Your Home, *Anne De Courcy, 1969*

**ILLUSTRATION 1** American electric
fitted kitchens, like this one, with their
plenitude of labour saving devices
and luxurious scale of refrigeration,
were the aspiration of British
homeowners in the early 1960s.

**ILLUSTRATION 2** Modern kitchens
of the mid to late 60s were
modularised and sturdily built, using
durable materials. They tended to
have few plug points, small cookers
and small fridges by modern
standards. They were often designed
in the 'Scandinavian humanist' style
and were usually planned in a close,
unified, relationship to the living and
dining areas, which were frequently
in the same room.

**ILLUSTRATION 3** It is only the size
of this room and the layout of the
furniture around the table that
identifies it as a kitchen in an older
and substantial house. Most of its
furniture and fittings are recognisably
of the modern fitted type. Such
rambling old kitchens captured the
imagination of the new
homeowners of the late 60s.

**ILLUSTRATION 3**
Homes and Gardens, *January 1964*

Reproduced courtesy of Homes and Gardens

**ILLUSTRATION 4**
Good Housekeeping's Home Encyclopaedia, *1968*

**ILLUSTRATION 4** Although this kitchen would have been luxurious for most people at the time, it is not architect-designed – its layout is not conceived in relation to other rooms but provides a straightforward arrangement of fittings and equipment. The units are modular but they are made as pieces of case furniture and painted in old-fashioned kitchen blue. New features here are the large worktop hob, the extractor and the separate built-in oven.

Private collection   Reproduced courtesy of Ideal Home / IPC Media

**ILLUSTRATION 5** This represents a top-of-the-range American-style kitchen in 1966. It has a diner-style breakfast bar, a double chest fridge (very rare in Britain at the time) and an island hob with floating extractor above. This type of kitchen was extremely expensive to build and equip. Kitchens were beginning to replace living rooms and bedrooms as the focus of most household expenditure.

**ILLUSTRATION 6**
Advertisement from Homes and Gardens, May 1964

**ILLUSTRATION 6** Fitted kitchens were more concerned with storage than accommodating appliances. When new machines, such as dishwashers, appeared they had no evolved place in the kitchen. The dishwasher, an expensive and high-status item, sat in a prominent position on a work surface.

**ILLUSTRATION 7** By the late 60s the efficient space- and labour-saving devices of the modern kitchen were generally desirable and quite widely available. But now, in response to the crisis in Modernism and the general nostalgia that was emerging, the fitted kitchen was being restyled in a 'Victorian country' idiom.

**ILLUSTRATION 7**
Kitchens: Plan Your Home, Anne De Courcy, 1969

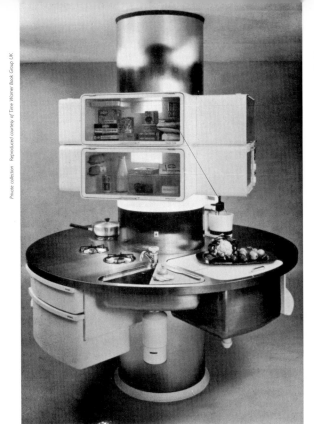

**ILLUSTRATION 8**

One Room Living, *Miriam Howitt, 1972*

**ILLUSTRATION 8** The modularisation and mass production of kitchen units led to designs for one-piece kitchens that adopted the imagery of space travel, particularly in their shiny, moulded appearance and the ingenious compactness of their storage. But such designs came at a time when the taste of homeowners in Britain was increasingly concerned with country kitchens and they were not popular.

**ILLUSTRATION 9** Before the development of truly modularised kitchens, Creda developed a hob system that allowed a bespoke kitchen to be made with a built-in hob. Such a system was used to fit out the 2,000 kitchens of the Barbican in the City of London.

**ILLUSTRATION 9**

One Room Living, *Miriam Howitt, 1972*

# FIREPLACES AND HEATING

*The vogue for open planning and extensive glazing made improvements in heating a necessary part of new house design. Central heating became much more widely available; in 1960 it was installed in only five per cent of homes but by 1971 this figure had risen to thirty-four per cent. Homes tended to have more heating appliances than previously and double glazing was introduced.*

*A bewildering number of heating systems developed, using a variety of energy sources. Because of its unobtrusive nature, under-floor heating was most attractive to architects and was a feature in many Modernist homes. Hot-air central heating was also quite widespread in later-60s architect-designed developments. But conventional hot-water heating gradually emerged as the standard system because it was easy to install and modify and could be run using a variety of fuel sources. In addition, the development of thermostatic controls and slimmer, less intrusive, radiators made hot-water systems more efficient.*

*Electric storage heaters were a cheaper option but they were bulky.*

*New Modern houses were often designed with central heating and without fireplaces; the kitchen or TV replaced the fire as the centre of the home. But the majority of homes, even those with central heating, had a source of direct heat in the living room. Coal fires remained popular. Models such as the BAXI were designed to burn more efficiently and often featured back boilers to provide water for radiators. Radiant gas fires were marketed as clean, modern replacements for coal fires. Popular throughout the decade, they provided a reassuring, instant and visible source of warmth and were frequently installed in the fireplaces of older accommodation. A wide range of Modernist-inspired fire surrounds was available. Their slim frames and recessed, pastel-coloured, flush surfaces emphasised the cleanliness of the modern appliances. Architects tended to favour open wood fires or the elegant, stainless steel tubes of Pither's anthracite stoves.*

BADDA 691  Reproduced courtesy of Ministerstone Ltd

**ILLUSTRATION I**

Catalogue for Minster hand-finished stone fireplaces, 1962

**ILLUSTRATION I** Traditional solid fuel fires had their last gasp in the 60s. They were commonly fitted in new homes up to about 1965 but after that they tended to be restricted to public housing in coal-producing areas. With their emphasis on horizontality and their cold hygienic colours, fireplace designs were really no different from those of the late 50s.

**ILLUSTRATION 2** Gas fires stepped into the breach left by coal fires; they were designed to slot straight into solid fuel fire surrounds. A strong selling point of gas fires was the familiar 'warmth' of the visible flames.

**ILLUSTRATION 2**

Catalogue, Home Heating and Hot Water by Gas, 1962

BADDA 907

**ILLUSTRATION 3** Central heating became more common in the late 60s. Its house-wide ambient warmth replaced localised radiant heaters (coal, electricity or gas) and was ideally suited to the open-plan design of Modern homes. Hot water radiators were the most popular form.

**Comfort is more than the papers on Sunday**

He's the engineer — She's the economist

**they both chose ConStor electric central heating THE WARM AIR WAY**

**ILLUSTRATION 4** Central heating and thermostatically controlled radiators changed patterns of living. With the idea of the all-over warm home came the promise of a new leisured and informal domestic life. There was no need for different summer and winter rooms or for the formality of dressing for different home experiences – jackets in the dining room and cardigans in the lounge had persisted into the early 60s. This was a new style of living that required fewer clothes to be worn indoors.

**ILLUSTRATION 5** The electrical appliance industry struggled to come up with a competitor for hot-water heating, which could not be run economically on electricity. The result was storage radiators, which were boxes filled with bricks heated by electricity. These were easy to install but took up a lot of space. They were often styled like furniture to counter the perception that they were a poor substitute for radiators.

# BATHROOMS

By 1971, eighty-eight per cent of homes had their own bathroom and there was the beginning of the trend toward multiple provision in affluent households. Purpose-built bathrooms were compact but, in the refurbished Victorian houses of the late 60s, large rooms were often converted for this purpose and the old roll-top baths made a reappearance.

At the beginning of the decade the bathroom was still, in general, a functional room, decorated in pastel colours and with linoleum flooring. But the advent of central heating meant that it could become a comfortable and pleasurable domestic space, furnished with features such as carpet, vinyl wallpaper, decorated tiles, a patterned shower screen and curtains.

The main technical innovation was a more widespread fitting of mixer taps and shower attachments or separate showers placed over the bath. Free-standing showers and shower rooms began to appear toward the end of the decade. Bidets were occasionally included in up-market bathrooms.

Stylistically, bathrooms followed similar trends to kitchens - the cool colours of the early-60s suites gave way, first of all, to white and then to colours like avocado, which complemented the orangey browns that appeared in kitchens. Toilet fittings took on a more coherent appearance with close-coupled designs and new plastic seats, which could be made in the same colour as the suite. Modernist designs of the early 60s, such as Ideal Standard's Studio Line, had clean curving lines with slim profiles, made possible by new ceramic materials. By the end of the decade, designs were more circular or rectangular in form.

The bath was generally set in a corner and panelled in, although, at the end of the 60s, it was sometimes adventurously set on a central dais. A bowl inset into the top of a unit or surface tended to supersede the pedestal basin of the early 60s.

**ILLUSTRATION I**
*Advertisement from* Homes and Gardens, *January 1964*

you'll always be proud of
bathroom walls faced with
'VITROLITE'

**ILLUSTRATION I** The bathroom shown in this advertisement differs little from an affluent bathroom of the 1930s. It is based on an aesthetic of hygiene rather than pleasure. Vitrolite was an opaque glass wall covering, introduced in the 1930s. It was still available in the mid 1960s but it was costly to install and its shiny finish was very dated in appearance.

**ILLUSTRATION 2** This bird's-eye view shows a standard Parker Morris bathroom of the later 60s - small, with little natural light, but warm and with efficient appliances. New bath and washbasin forms were developed to maximise the capacity of the small service rooms that typified the modern open-plan house. Mirror-fronted cabinets increased the sense of space while dark paint colours gave a sense of cosiness. This bathroom is very different from the baroque excesses of the counter culture, as seen in illustration 6.

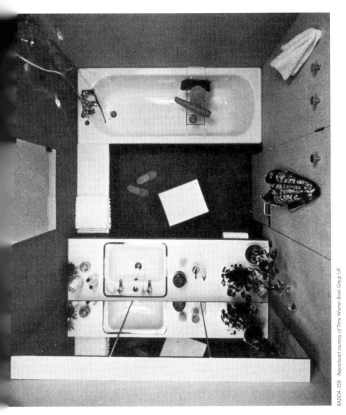

**ILLUSTRATION 2**

Storage, *Geoffrey Salmon, 1967*

**ILLUSTRATION 3**

Catalogue for Twyfords, 1966

**ILLUSTRATION 3** The Parker Morris report recommended that a separate toilet room should include a hand basin. The inclusion of this additional item in an already small room led to the need for smaller washbasins. This particularly extreme design was used at the Barbican development in London, where space was so tight that the basin was fitted into the wall. Despite technical difficulties, the design adhered to the rationalist rectilinearity of early-60s architectural aesthetics.

*Private collection*

**ILLUSTRATION 4** The treatment
of the bathroom as a styled room
rather than simply a wet service
area was encouraged by the
introduction of waterproof vinyl
wallpapers. In this example the
cold, rather 50s, blue of the
bathroom suite is softened by
the matching 18th-century-revival
fabrics and wallpapers. This was
a very conservative design
for 1968.

**ILLUSTRATION 6**

English Style, *Mary Gilliat, 1967*

Private collection

**ILLUSTRATION 5** By the late 60s new, fashionable, designs entered the market, usually from Italy, enabling the bathroom to look as 'architect-designed' as the kitchen or living area. A shower over the bath and an enclosing glass screen was a feature of this decade – the general adoption of separate shower cubicles came later. This example, with its fitted basin and geometric tiles on the ceiling and walls, looks forward to the Italian-inspired style of the 70s.

**ILLUSTRATION 6** With the advent of central heating and waterproof carpets, bathrooms became warm, comfortable places that could be decorated in any style. In the later 60s, when the Hippie generation began moving into old Victorian houses, they used new paints and materials to turn the bathroom into a key symbol of the hedonism of the counter culture.

# FURTHER READING

*Living Rooms – 20th-Century Interiors at the Geffrye Museum* Lesley Hoskins (1998)

*New Houses* Penelope Whiting (1964)

*Sixties Design* Philippe Garner (1996)

*The Ideal Home through the 20th Century* Deborah Ryan (1997)

*The Place of Home. English Domestic Environments, 1914-2000* Alison Ravetz (1995)

*The Sixties: decade of design revolution* Lesley Jackson (1998)

*Op to Pop : Furniture of the 1960s* Cara Greenberg (1999)

*Decorative Art 1960s* Charlotte & Peter Fiell (2000)

# PLACES TO VISIT

**MoDA** (The Museum of Domestic Design & Architecture), Middlesex University, Cat Hill, Barnet, Hertfordshire EN4 8HT Telephone 020 8411 5244 www.moda.mdx.ac.uk
MoDA's collections of trade catalogues, home magazines, designs, wallpapers and textiles can be viewed by appointment in MoDA's study room.

**BARBARA HEPWORTH MUSEUM AND SCULPTURE GARDEN,** Barnoon Hill, St Ives, Cornwall, TR26 1AD
Telephone 01736 796226
Administered by Tate Gallery St Ives
Barbara Hepworth lived in this cottage from 1959 until her death in 1975 and the small house and garden are representative of Modernist home design in the early 1960s.

**DESIGN MUSEUM,** Shad Thames, London, SE1 2YD  Telephone 0870 833 9955
www.designmuseum.org
The museum has a permanent display containing many classic designs of the 60s and also has a good archive.

**GEFFRYE MUSEUM,** Kingsland Road, London, E2 8EA Telephone 020 7739 9893
www.geffrye-museum.org.uk
The museum displays include an open-plan living room of about 1960.

**THE GIBBERD GARDEN,** Marsh Lane, Gilden Way, Harlow, Essex, CM17 0NA
Telephone 01279 442112
Sir Frederick Gibberd, master planner of Harlow New Town and architect of Liverpool Catholic Cathedral, lived here from the late 50s until his death in 1984. His garden has been described by Hugh Johnson as 'One of the few outstanding examples of 20th-century garden design'.

**PICKER ONE,** South West London
Telephone 020 8942 8811
Built in 1968, the house was commissioned by a wealthy American-born businessman and exemplifies the design ethos of the period. Habitat was responsible for the interior design and furnishing. A separate gallery, built in 1977, houses an important collection of modern art.
The house is open on certain days during the spring and summer months for guided tours, which must be booked in advance with the curator.

**MoDA** is known as the 'museum of the history of the home'. Its varied exhibitions give a vivid picture of domestic life during the first half of the twentieth century whilst also looking at contemporary design and other issues related to the domestic environment.

Gallery talks, events, practical workshops and study days provide educational, informative and entertaining experiences for adults and children.

MoDA holds six collections and a dedicated Study Room allows access to items not on display.

### SILVER STUDIO COLLECTION

The archive of a commercial pattern design practice active between 1880 and 1963. Its many thousands of designs, wallpapers and textile samples span the popular styles of the period.

### CROWN WALLPAPER COLLECTION

Wallpaper books mainly from the 1950s, represent the colourful and engaging patterns of that time.

### DOMESTIC DESIGN COLLECTION

More than 4,000 books, magazines and trade catalogues relating to design for the home and household management (1850-1960).

### SIR JM RICHARDS LIBRARY

Books and journals collected by Sir JM Richards (1907-1992), a leading architectural writer. The collection covers architecture, interiors, furniture, landscape and town planning.

### PEGGY ANGUS ARCHIVE

The entire contents of the London studio of Peggy Angus (1904-1993), an artist, teacher and designer of tiles and bespoke hand-printed wallpapers.

### CHARLES HASLER COLLECTION

An archive relating to the work of Charles Hasler (1908-1992), a typographer and graphic designer who played a significant role in many high-profile exhibitions, poster campaigns and in book publishing from the mid-1930s to the mid-1980s.